YOU CAN TEACH YOURSELF®

UKE

by William Bay

This book is available either by itself or packaged with a companion audio and/or video recording. If you have purchased the book only, you may wish to purchase the recordings separately. The publisher strongly recommends using a recording along with the text to assure accuracy of interpretation and make learning easier and more enjoyable.

CD CONTENTS

1. Tune Up
2. Three Blind Mice/Page 11
3. Skip To My Lou/Page 12
4. Rock-A-My Soul/Page 13
5. Polly Wolly Doodle/Page 13
6. Oh, My Darling Clementine/Page 14
7. Pay Me My Money Down/Page 15
8. Buffalo Gals/Page 17
9. He's Got The Whole Word In His Hands/Page18
10. Santa Lucia/Page 20
11. Our Boys Will Shine Tonight/Page 22
12. The Marine's Hymn/Page 23
13. Everytime I Feel The Spirt/Page 25
14. Standing In The Need Of Prayer/Page 25
15. Aloha Oe/Page 27
16. Moonlight Bay/Page 28
17. Go Tell It On The Mountain/Page 29
18. Battle Hymn Of The Republic/Page 30
19. Away In A Manger/Page31
20. This Little Light Of Mine/Page 31
21. Peace Like A River/Page 32
22. The Wabash Cannonball/Page 33
23. Down By The Riverside/Page 34
24. She'll Be Coming Round The Mountain/Page 35
25. When The Saints Go Marchin' In/Page 38
26. Streets Of Laredo/Page 39
27. Oh! Susanna/Page 41
28. Frankie & Johnny/Page 42
29. Juanita/Page 44
30. Mary Ann/Page 47
31. Beautiful Brown Eyes/Page 48
32. Fascination/Page 49
33. Chinatown My Chinatown/Page 50
34. Ida, Sweet As Apple Cider/Page 51
35. When Irish Eyes Are Smiling/Page 52
36. By The Light Of The Silvery Moon/Page 53
37. The Darktown Strutter's Ball/Page 54
38. That's An Irish Lullaby/Page 55
39. Meet Me In St. Louis/Page 56
40. Shine On, Harvest Moon/Page 59
41. The Sidewalks Of New York/Page 60
42. Bill Bailey, Won't You Please Come Home?/Page 64
43. For Me & My Gal/Page 65
44. Oh, You Beautiful Doll/Page 66
45. I Want A Girl Just Like The Girl Who Married Dear Old Dad/Page 68
46. Hello, Ma Baby/Page 71
47. Alexander's Ragtime Band/Page 73
48. I Love You Truly/Page 75
49. Alabama Jubilee/Page 78
50. Peg O' My Heart/Page 80
51. Ballin' The Jack/Page 81
52. In The Good Old Summertime/Page 82
53. The Yankee Doodle Boy/Page 83
54. My Gal Sal/Page 84
55. My Wild Irish Rose/Page 85
56. Take Me Out To The Ballgame/Page 87
57. The Blue Bells Of Scotland/Page 89
58. Pretty Baby/Page 92
59. My Melancholy Baby/Page 93

2 3 4 5 6 7 8 9 0

Visit us on the Web at www.melbay.com — E-mail us at email@melbay.com

Contents

How To Hold The Uke 3

Parts Of The Uke 4

Ways To Tune Your Uke 5

Strumming Your Uke 7

The Left Hand 8

How To Read Chord Diagrams 9

Playing The C Chord 10

Time Signatures 10

Our First Songs 11

A New Chord 12

Down-Up Strum 17

The F Chord 19

Two New Chords 26

Chords In The Key Of D 36

Chords In The Key Of F 43

More Advanced Songs

    Key Of C 49

    Key Of G 58

    Key Of F 70

    Key Of B♭ 78

    Key Of D 89

Basic Uke Chord Chart 94

Index Of Songs 96

How To Hold The Uke

Standing

REMEMBER TO:
1 Hold the uke above your waist.
2 Hold it at a slight upward angle.
3 Use your right forearm to press the uke against your body.
4 Relax!

Sitting

Parts Of The Uke

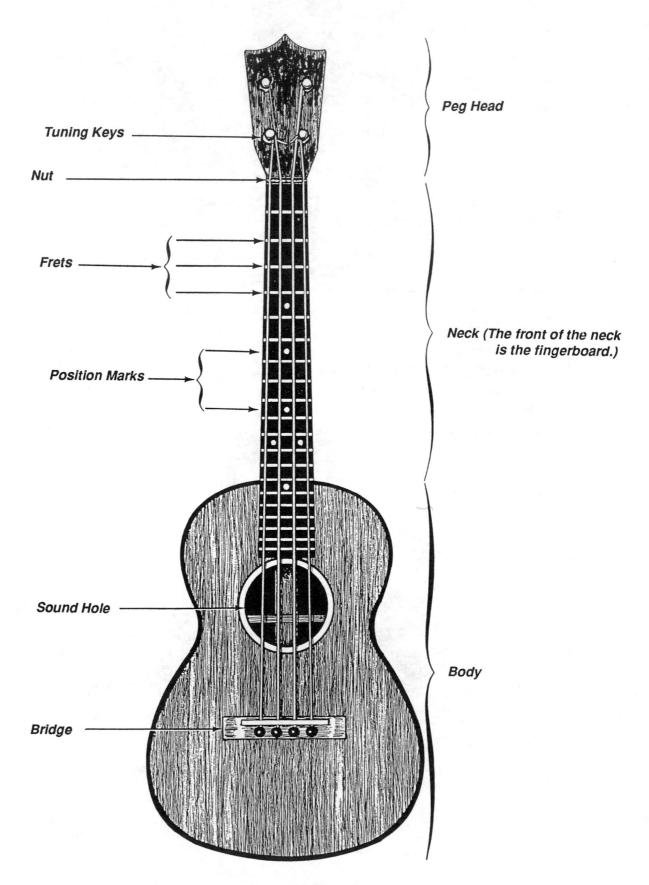

Peg Head

Tuning Keys

Nut

Frets

Position Marks

Neck (The front of the neck is the fingerboard.)

Sound Hole

Body

Bridge

Ways To Tune Your Uke

1. Tune It To A Piano

This method will use *"C tuning."* In C tuning the strings are tuned to the following notes:

First String . . . . A ①
Second String . . . . . . E ②
Third String . . . . C ③
Fourth String . . . . . . G ④

On a piano the notes are found as follows:

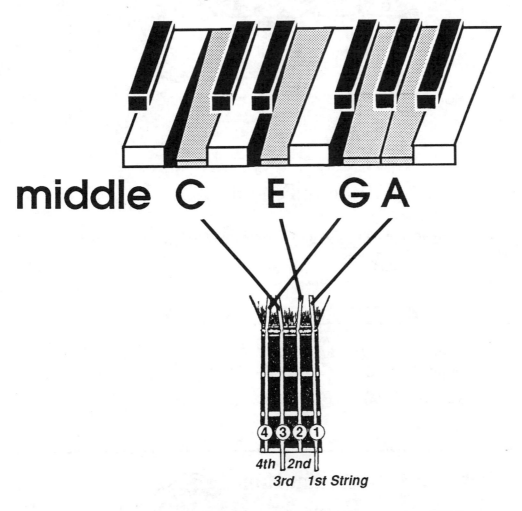

middle **C** **E** **G A**

4th 2nd
3rd   1st String

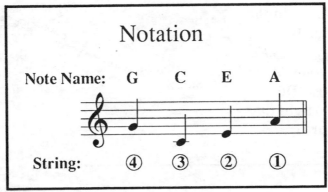

Notation

Note Name:	G	C	E	A
String:	④	③	②	①

2. Tuning With A Pitch Pipe

Ukulele pitch pipes can be purchased from most music stores. Blow into the appropriate sound hole and tune the string to the correct pitch.

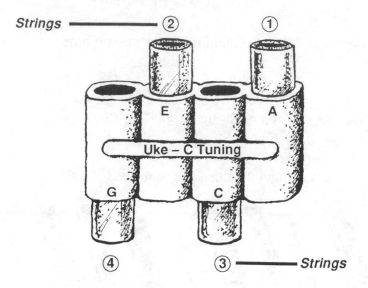

3. Tuning By Ear

Once you tune your first string to a pitch that sounds correct (not too high or too low), you can use the following expression:

	My	dog	has	fleas.
Note:	G	C	E	A
String:	④	③	②	①

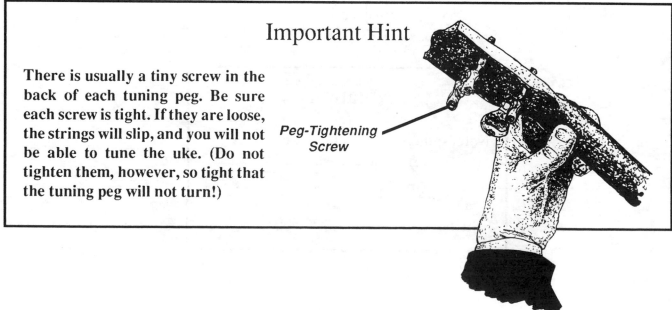

Important Hint

There is usually a tiny screw in the back of each tuning peg. Be sure each screw is tight. If they are loose, the strings will slip, and you will not be able to tune the uke. (Do not tighten them, however, so tight that the tuning peg will not turn!)

Peg-Tightening Screw

Strumming Your Uke

1. Using A Pick

Picks can be purchased at your local music store. It is usually desirable to use a "felt" pick. This will give your uke a soft, mellow tone. Plastic picks will give a sharper, more brittle tone. If a plastic pick is to be used, try to find a thin, very flexible one.

Felt Pick

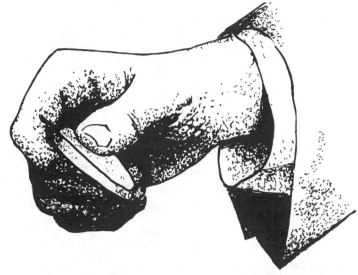

Holding The Pick (Right Hand)

2. Using Your Thumb

You can also strum your uke with your right-hand thumb.

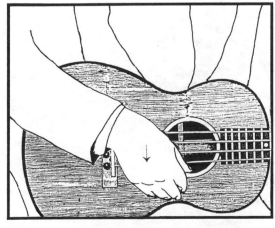

Down Strum ↓

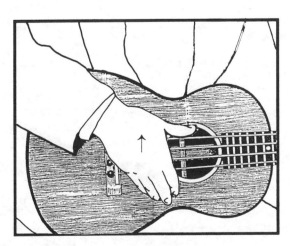

Up Strum ↑

The Left Hand

The following illustrations show the proper positioning of the left hand. Notice that only the *tips* of the left-hand fingers are used to press down the strings. (Be sure your fingers do not accidentally touch the adjacent string. If this happens, the adjacent string will sound muffled or deadened.) Be sure the thumb is on the back of the neck, *not* wrapped around the side. Finally, when you press down a string, place your finger behind the metal fret, *not* on top of it.

Correct

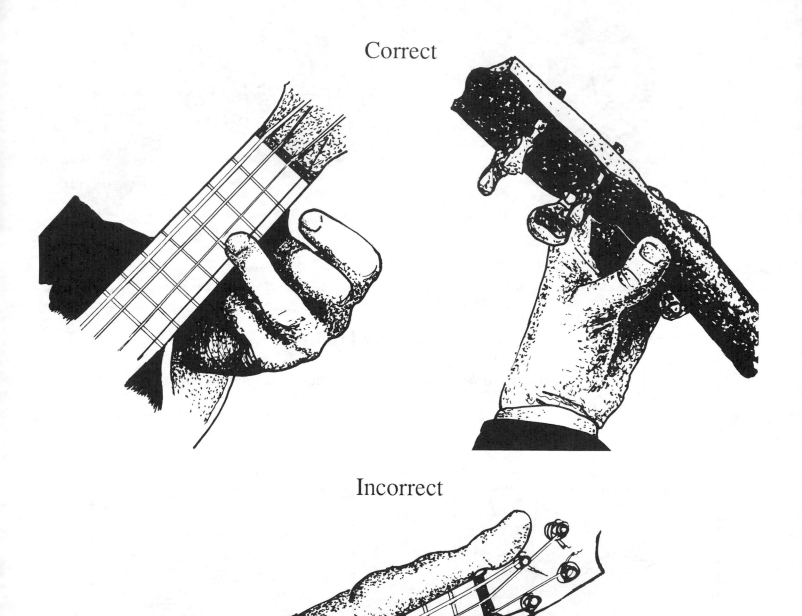

Incorrect

How To Read Chord Diagrams

A chord diagram shows you where to place your fingers in order to play a chord. The vertical lines are the strings. The horizontal lines are the frets. The circled numbers are left-hand fingers.

Left-hand fingers are numbered as follows:

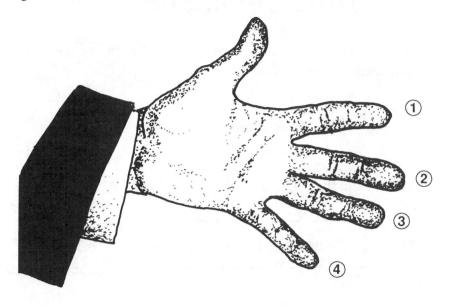

Our First Chord
C

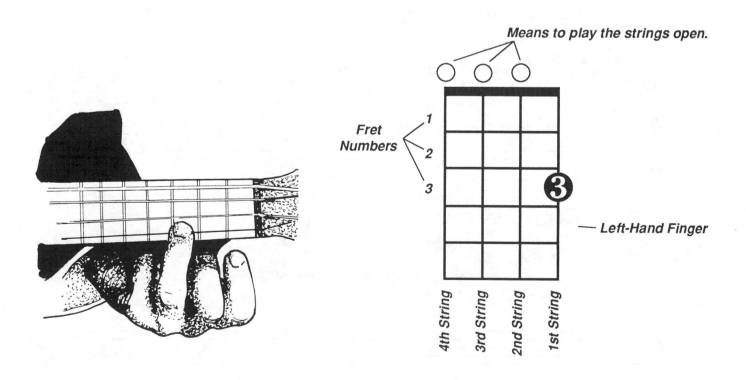

Playing The C Chord

Practice strumming the C chord until it sounds clear.

Time Signatures

Every song has a time signature. The time signature appears at the beginning of every song and tells you how many beats or counts are in each measure.

$\frac{4}{4}$ or **C** = "Common Time"

Hold the C chord and play as follows.

Remember: / = Down Strum

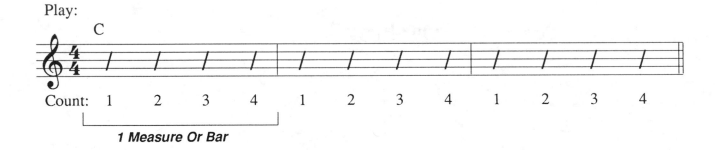

$\frac{3}{4}$ = **Three-Four Or "Waltz" Time**

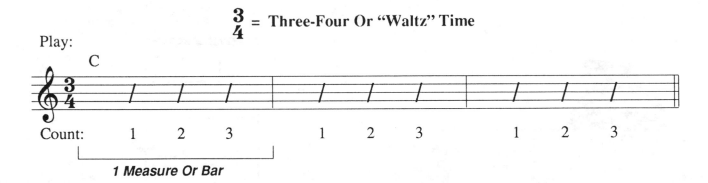

$\frac{2}{4}$ = **Two-Four Or "March" Time**

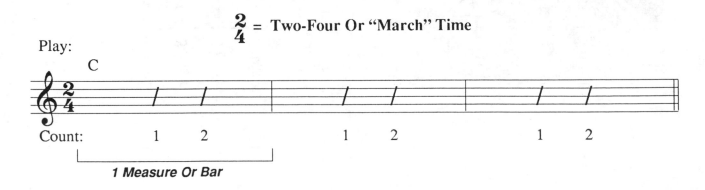

Our First Songs

Reading Music

Three Blind Mice

Row, Row, Row Your Boat

A New Chord

G7

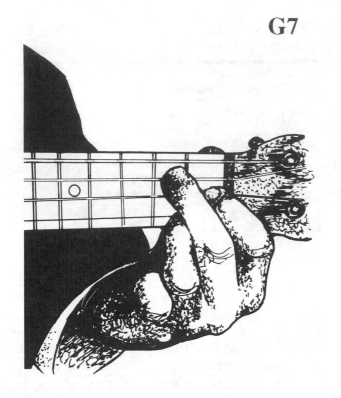

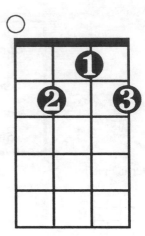

Starting pitch

Skip To My Lou

C	G7
Left and Right, Oh skip to my Lou	Left and Right, Oh skip to my Lou
C	G7 C
Left and Right, Oh skip to my Lou	Skip to my Lou my darling.

Rock-A-My Soul

Polly Wolly Doodle

Oh, My Darling Clementine

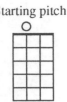

In a cav-ern in a can-yon ex-ca-va-ting for a

mine - Dwelt a min-er, for-ty nin-er and his daugh-ter Clem-en-tine.

Oh my dar-ling, oh my dar-ling, oh my dar-ling Clem-en-

tine, - You are lost and gone for-ev-er I am sor-ry Clem-en-tine.

Three Fishermen

vs. 2. First one's name was Abraham
(Repeat)
Abra, Abra, ham, ham, ham
(Repeat)
First one's name was Abraham

vs. 4. Third one's name was Jacob
Jakey, Jakey, cub, cub, cub.

vs. 3. Second's name was Isaac.
Isy, Isy, ac, ac, ac.

vs. 5. Wish they'd gone to Amsterdam.
Amster, Amster, dam, dam, dam.

Pay Me Money Down

2. I thought I heard the captain say,
Pay me my money down.
Tomorrow is our sailing day,
Pay me my money down.
Chorus

Down-Up Strum

/ = Down Strum
V = Up Strum

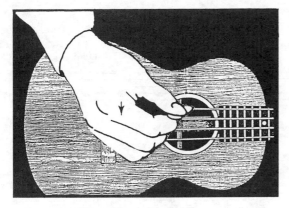

Down Strum /

Up Strum V

Buffalo Gals

He's Got The Whole World

Starting pitch

2. He's got the little bitsy baby. . . .   3. He's got you and me brother. . . . .

Hey Lolly

Starting pitch

C
1. Wake up in the mornin', sunny **and** bright
            G7
   Hey lolly, lolly lo.
   Looked in the mirror, got a terrible fright!
            C
   Hey lolly, lolly lo.
   C
2. I have a girl she's ten feet tall,
            G7
   Hey lolly, lolly lo.
   Sleeps on the floor with her feet in the hall,
            C
   Hey lolly, lolly lo.

[make up your own verses]

The F Chord

Master the following chord study:

Repeat until no time is lost in changing.

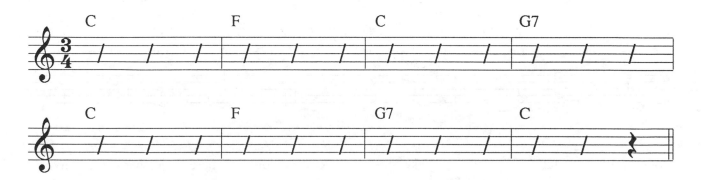

The C, F, and G7 chords are the principal chords in the key of C.

Santa Lucia

Yellow Rose Of Texas

Swanee River

Wildwood Flower

Our Boys Will Shine Tonight

The Marine's Hymn

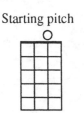

Starting pitch

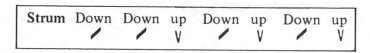

Camptown Races

Railroad Bill

Every Time I Feel The Spirit

Starting pitch

Syncopated Strum   Down   Down   up   up   Down   up

hold

Chorus: Ev - ry   time I   feel the spirit **mov-in'** in my **heart** I will pray, ev' - ry

time I   feel The spi - rit mov - 'in in my heart I will pray. [Verse:] U - pon the

moun-tain, when my Lord spoke, out of his mouth came fire and smoke; Look'd all a -

round **me** it looked so fine 'til I asked my Lord if all were mine.

Standing In The Need Of Prayer

Starting pitch

Shuffle Strum Down up Down up Down up Down up

Ain't my broth-er or my sis-ter but it's me, oh, Lord, stand-ing in the need of

prayer, Ain't my broth-er or my sis-ter but it's me, oh, Lord, stand-ing in the need of

prayer. It's me, it's me, oh, Lord, stand-ing in the need of

prayer, it's me, it's me, oh, Lord, stand-ing in the need of prayer

Two New Chords

The D7 Chord

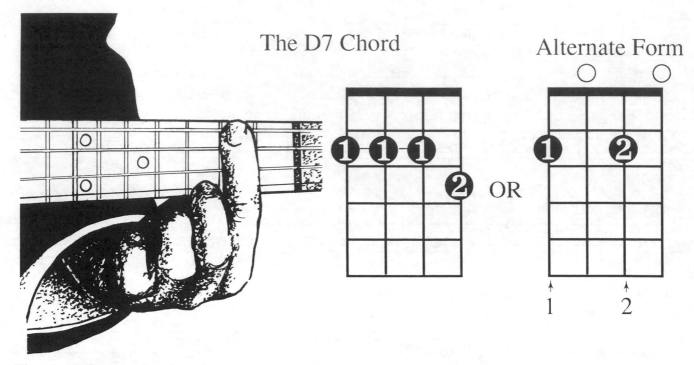

Alternate Form

OR

Play the following chord study:

C   D7   G7   C

(repeat)

The G Chord

The chords in the key of G are: G, C, and D7.

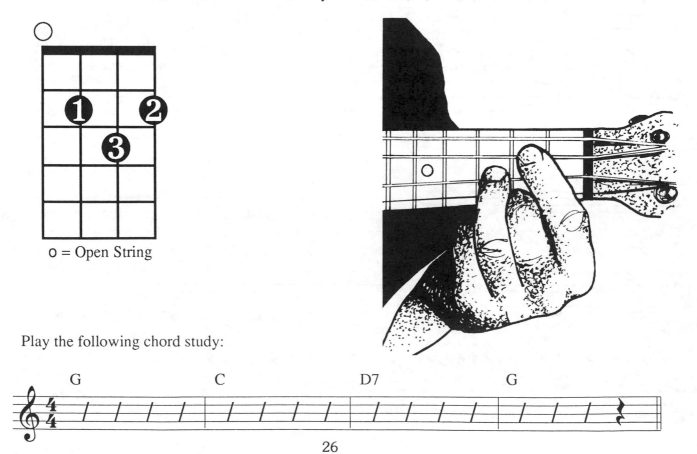

o = Open String

Play the following chord study:

G   C   D7   G

Aloha Oe
(Farewell To Thee)

Moonlight Bay

Go Tell It On The Mountain

Battle Hymn Of The Republic

Starting pitch

2. I have seen Him in the watch fires of a hundred circling camps.
   They have builded Him an altar in the evening dews and damps.
   I have read His righteous sentence by the dim of flaring lamps,
   His truth is marching on.

3. In the beauty of the lilies, Christ was born across the sea,
   With a glory in His bosom that transfigures you and me;
   As He died to make men holy, Let us die to make men free,

   While God is marching on.

Away In A Manger

This Little Light Of Mine

Peace Like A River

Starting pitch

Strum: Down Down Down up Down up

G
1. I've got peace like a riv-er, I've got peace like a riv-er, I've got

C

G ... **D7** ... **G**
peace like a riv-er in my soul; I've got peace like a riv-er I've got

C ... **G** ... **D7** ... **G**
peace like a riv-er, I've got peace like a riv-er in my soul.

2. I've got joy like a fountain   3. I've got love like an **ocean**.

All Through The Night

Starting pitch

Slowly

Strum: Down Down Down up

G **C** **D7** **C** **D7** **G**
Sleep, my child, and peace at-tend thee. All through the night.
Guar-dian an-gels, God will send thee all through the night.

(Repeat)

C ... **D7**
Soft and drow-sy hours are creep-ing, hill and vale in slum-ber sleep-ing

G **C** **D7** **C** **D7** **G**
I am lov-ing vig-il keep-ing all through the night.

        G   C   D7   C D7   G
2. While the moon her watch is keeping, all through the night.
        G   C   D7   C D7   G
While the weary world is sleeping, all through the night.
        C
O'er thy spirit gently stealing,
                D7
Visions of delight revealing,
        G   C   D7   C D7   G
Breathes a pure and holy feeling, all through the night.

Blow, Ye Winds

The Wabash Cannonball

Down By The Riverside

2. I'm gonna join hands with everyone, etc.
3. I'm gonna put on my long white robe, etc.
4. I'm gonna talk with the **Prince of Peace**, etc.

She'll Be Coming Round The Mountain

The Gospel Train

2. The fare is cheap and all can go,
   C   D7
   The rich and poor are there;
   G   G7   C
   No second class aboard this train,
   G   D7   G G7
   No difference in the fare. Chorus

3. I hear that train a-comin',
   C   D7
   She sure is speedin' fast,
   G   G7   C
   So get your tickets ready
   G   D7   G G7
   And ride to heaven at last. Chorus

35

Chords In The Key Of D

The three primary chords in the key of D are: D, G, and A7.

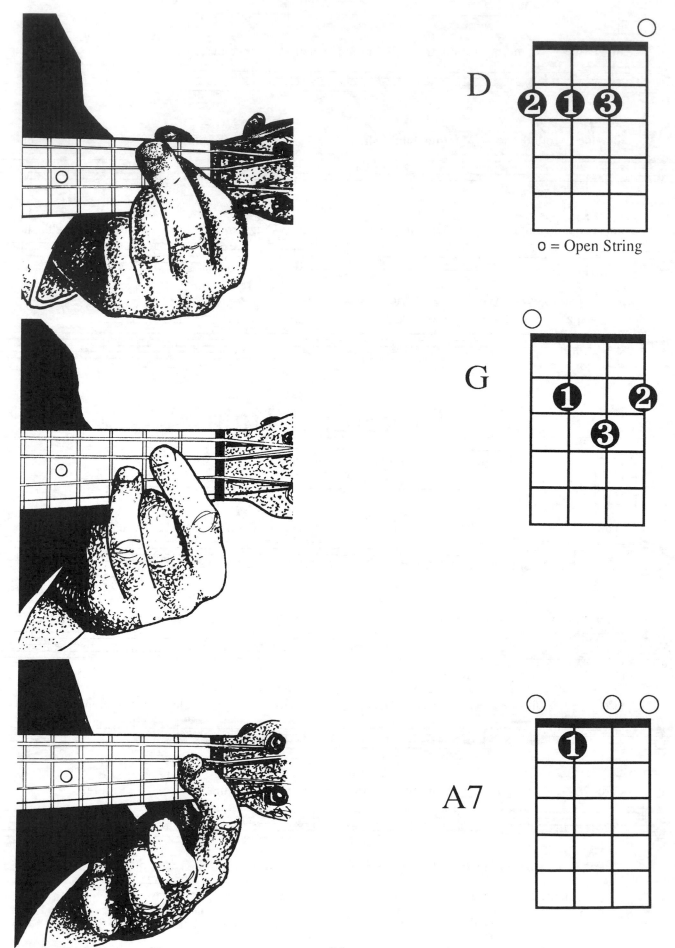

D

o = Open String

G

A7

She Wore A Yellow Ribbon

American
Folk Song

Bright Tempo

Chorus:

D
But, in her heart, she has a secret passion
                           A7
She has it in the springtime, and in the month of May;
    D
And if you asked her who is now her passion,
                              A7   D
She has it for a college man who's not so far away.
    Chorus

When The Saints Go Marchin' In

Starting pitch

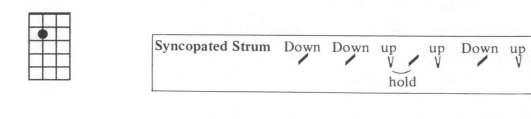

2. And when they gather 'round the throne.
3. And when they crown him **King** of kings
4. And on that Hallelujah day.

Streets Of Laredo

Starting pitch

2. "Go fetch me a cup, a cup of cold water,
To cool my parched lips," the cowboy then said;
Before I returned, the spirit had left him
And gone to its Maker - the cowboy was dead.

3. We beat the drum slowly and played the fife lowly,
And bitterly wept as we bore him along;
For we all loved our comrade, so brave, young, and handsome,
We all loved our comrade although he'd done wrong.

Crawdad Song

Starting pitch

The Girl I Left Behind Me

Starting pitch

Strum	Down	Rest	Down	up

D ... **G** ... **A7** ... **D**

I am lone-some since I crossed the hill and o'er the moor and val - ley, such a

G ... **A7** ... **D**

heav - y thought my heart do fill since part - ing with my__ Las - sie. I__

A7

seek no more the joy in life, for ech - oes but re - mind me how__

D ... **G** ... **A7** ... **D**

swift the hours did pass a - way with the girl I left be - hind me.

Li'l Liza Jane

Starting pitch

Strum	Down	Rest	Down	up	Down	up	Down	up

D ... **G** ... **D**

I got a gal and you got none Li'l Liz - a Jane,

A7 ... **D**

I got a gal that calls me hon; Li'l Liz - a Jane.

D ... **G** **D** ... **G** **D** ... **A7**

Chorus Oh E - liz - a, Li'l Liz - a Jane,

D ... **G** **D** ... **A7** ... **D**

Oh E - liz - a, Li'l Liz - a Jane.

40

Oh! Susanna

Come And Go With Me

2. There'll be singin' in that land
4. There is freedom in that land

3. There'll be dancin' in that land.
5. There is love in that land.

Frankie & Johnny

Chords In The Key of F

The three primary chords in the key of F are: F, B♭, and C7.

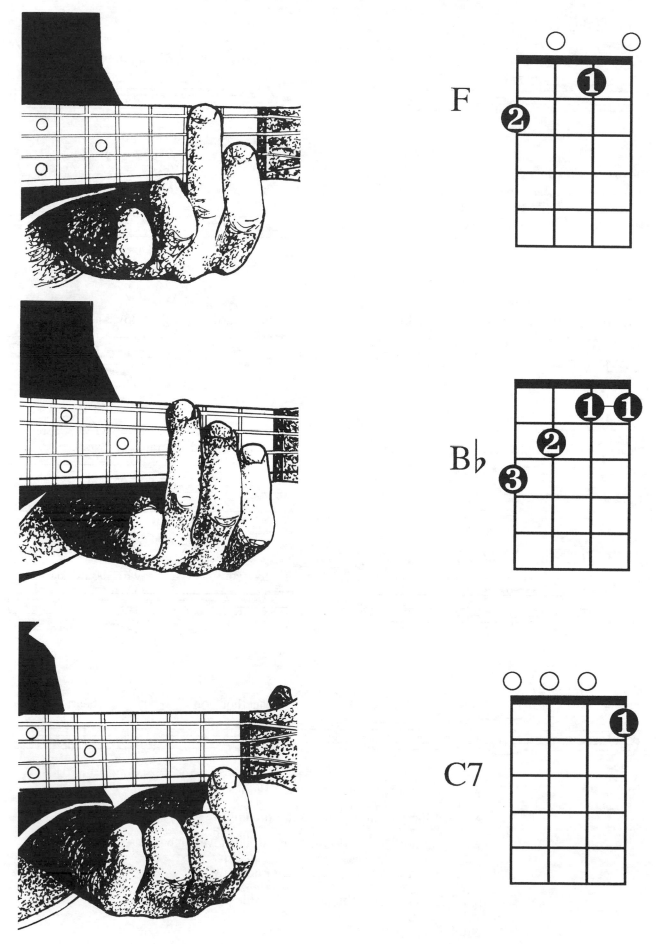

F

B♭

C7

Juanita

2. When in thy dreaming moons like these shall shine again,
   And daylight beaming prove thy dreams are vain,
   Wilt thou not, relenting, for thine absent lover sigh?
   In thy heart consenting to a prayer gone by?
   Nita! Juanita! Let me linger by thy side!
   Nita! Juanita! Be my own fair bride.

Swing Low, Sweet Chariot

Starting pitch

Strum: Down Down Down Down up

2. When I get to glory, my voice I'll raise,
   Comin' for to carry me home,
   To sing a song of grateful praise,
   Comin' for to carry me home.

45

Starting pitch

Sweet By And By

Strum: Down Down up Down up Down up
/ / V / V / V

Gospel Song

There's a land that is fair — er than day, and by

faith we can see it a – far, for the Fa — ther waits o — ver the

way, To pre – pare us a dwell — ing place there.

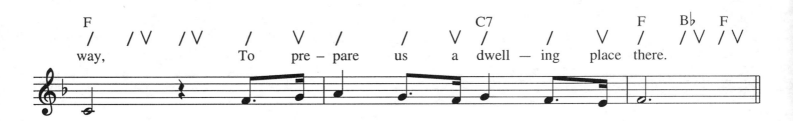

Chorus In the sweet by and by, We shall meet on that beau – ti – ful shore, In the

sweet by and by, We shall meet on that beau – ti – ful shore.

        F   Bb   F
2. We shall sing on that beautiful shore
                 C7
    The melodious songs of the blest;
            F   Bb   F
    And our spirits shall sorrow no more
                 C7   F Bb F
    Not a sigh for the blessing of rest.

Chorus

                    F   Bb   F
3. To our beautiful Father above
                      C7
    We will offer our tribute of praise,
                 F   Bb   F
    For the glorious gift of his love
                      C7   F Bb F
    And the blessings that hallow our days.

Chorus

This Train

Mary Ann

Beautiful Brown Eyes

Goin' Down The Road Feelin' Bad

Fascination

CHORDS Needed:

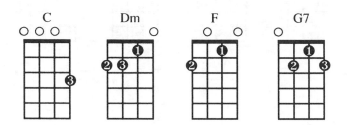

Starting pitch
(down 1 8ve)

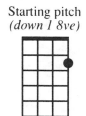

Suggested Strum: Down Down Down up

(no chord) C
It was fas - ci - na - tion, my dear,_____ I was in a

par - a - dise when you were near,_____ I was all a - glow,_____

___ more than you could know;_____ I was just a dream, now I see things more

F G7 *(no chord)* C
clear - ly,_____ It was fas - ci - na - tion, that's true,_____ there I was en -

Dm
tranced by the star - light and you,_____ Then you turned a - way, love, and

G7 Dm G7 C
oh, when you left me,_____ fas - ci - na - tion van - ished too._____

Chinatown, My Chinatown

CHORDS Needed:

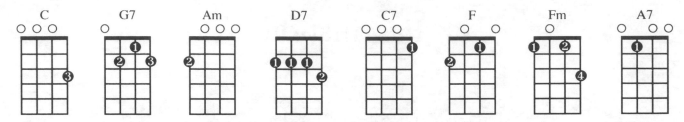

Starting pitch

Suggested Strum: | Down up Down up | up Down up |

C
Chi - na - town, my Chi - na - town,_____ Where the lights are

G7
low,_____ Hearts that know no oth - er land,_____

Am
D7
Drift - ing

to and fro,_____ Dream - y, dream - y Chi - na - town,_____
G7   C

Al - mond eyes of brown,_____ Hearts seem light and
C7   F   Fm

life seems bright_____ In dream - y Chi - na - town._____
C   A7   D7   G7   C

Ida, Sweet As Apple Cider

When Irish Eyes Are Smiling

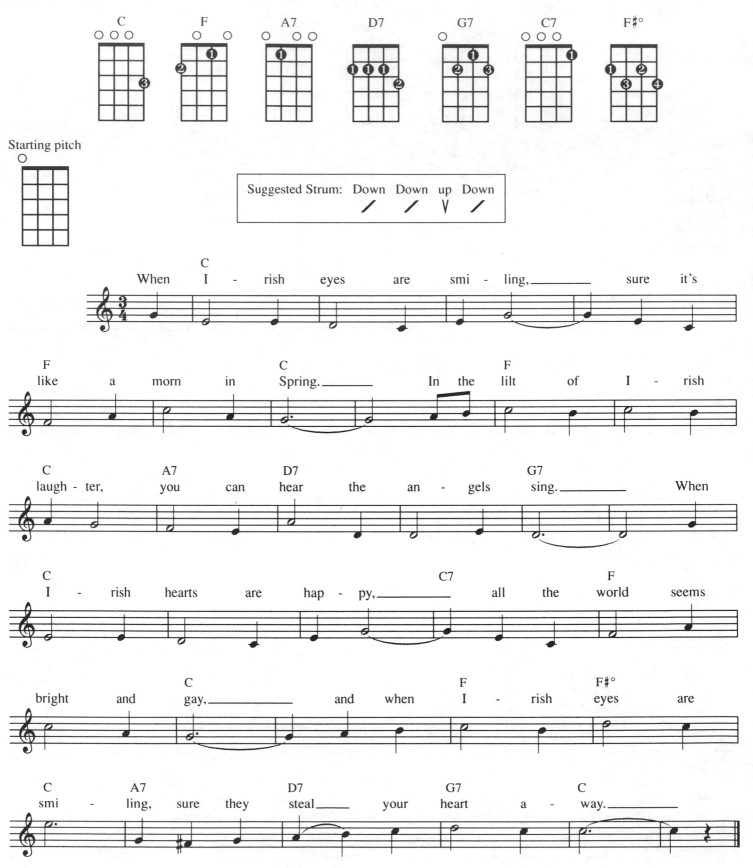

By the Light of the Silvery Moon

CHORDS Needed:

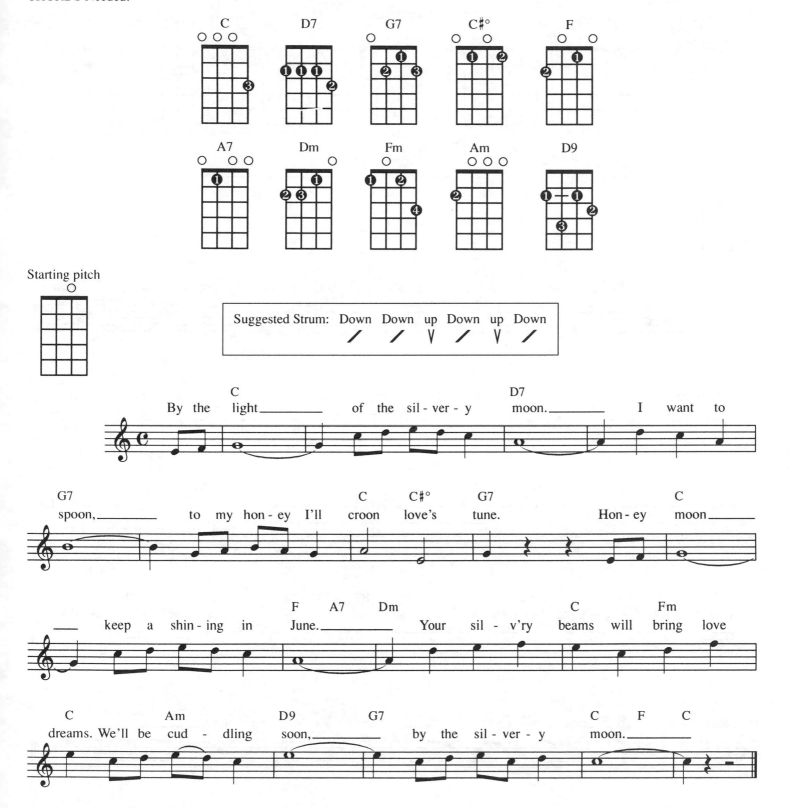

The Darktown Strutters' Ball

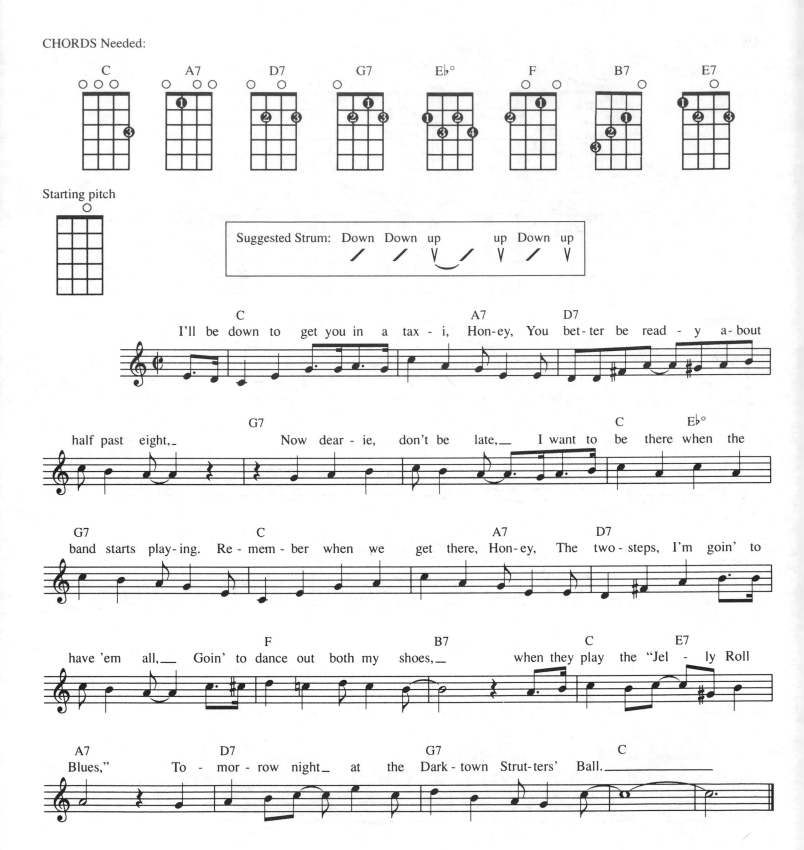

That's An Irish Lullaby

CHORDS Needed:

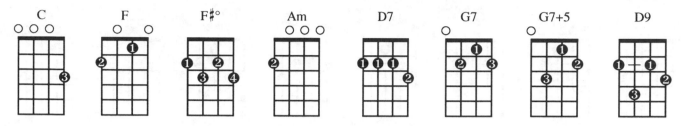

Starting pitch

Suggested Strum: Down Down

Slowly

Too - ra-loo - ra-loo-ral,_____ Too - ra-loo - ra - li,

Too - ra-loo - ra - loo-ral,_____ Hush now, don't you cry!_____

Too - ra-loo - ra - loo-ral,_____ Too - ra-loo - ra - li,

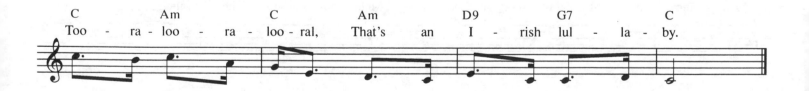

Too - ra-loo - ra - loo-ral, That's an I - rish lul - la - by.

Meet Me In St. Louis, Louis

CHORDS Needed:

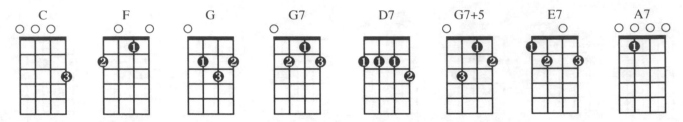

Starting pitch

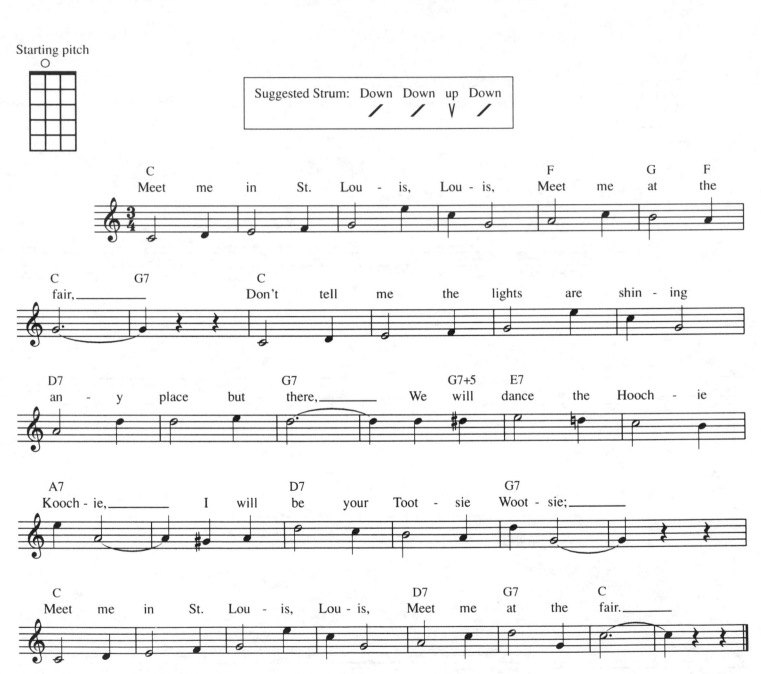

Dear Old Girl

CHORDS Needed:

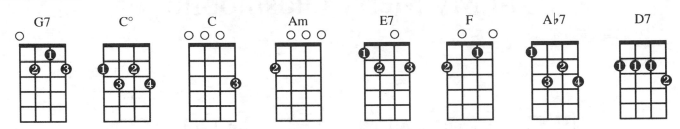

G7   C°   C   Am   E7   F   A♭7   D7

Starting pitch

Suggested Strum: Down Down up Down up Down

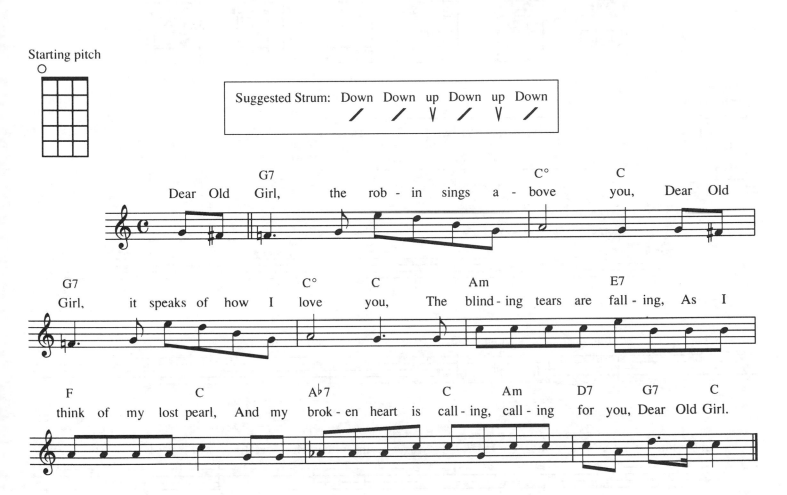

Dear Old Girl, the rob - in sings a - bove you, Dear Old Girl, it speaks of how I love you, The blind - ing tears are fall - ing, As I think of my lost pearl, And my brok - en heart is call - ing, call - ing for you, Dear Old Girl.

In My Merry Oldsmobile

CHORDS Needed:

Shine On Harvest Moon

CHORDS Needed:

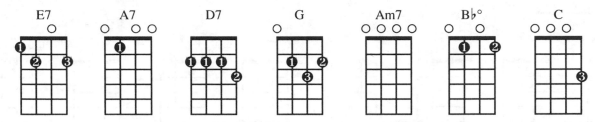

E7   A7   D7   G   Am7   B♭°   C

Starting pitch

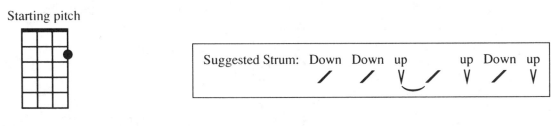

Suggested Strum: Down   Down   up   up   Down   up

E7 .... A7
Oh, shine on, shine on har-vest moon,_____ up in the sky.

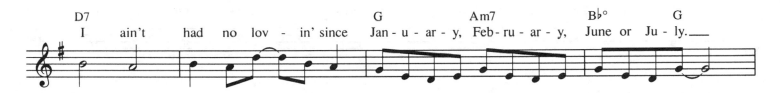

D7 .... G   Am7 .... B♭° ...... G
I ain't had no lov - in' since Jan - u - ar - y, Feb - ru - ar - y, June or Ju - ly.___

E7 .... A7
Snow time ain't no time to stay_____ out- doors and spoon.   So

D7 .... G   C .... G
shine on, shine on har - vest moon, for me and my gal.___

The Sidewalks of New York
[East Side, West Side]

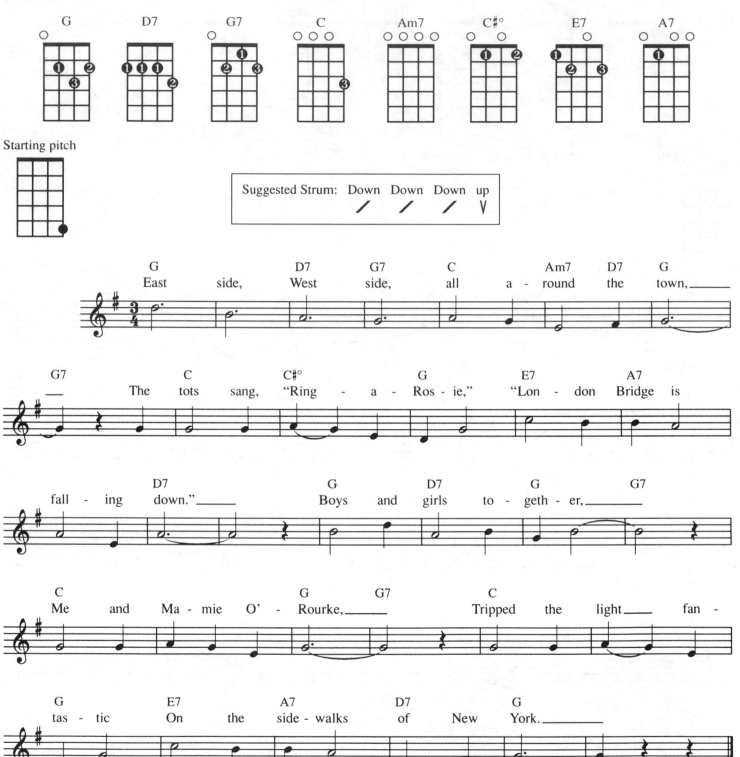

Wait Till The Sun Shines, Nellie

CHORDS Needed:

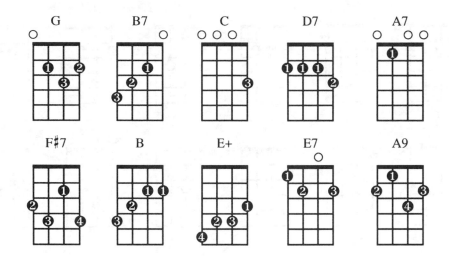

Starting pitch

Suggested Strum: Down Down Down up Down up

Down By The Old Mill Stream

While Strolling Through The Park One Day

Bill Bailey, Won't You Please Come Home?

For Me And My Gal

Oh, You Beautiful Doll

CHORDS Needed:

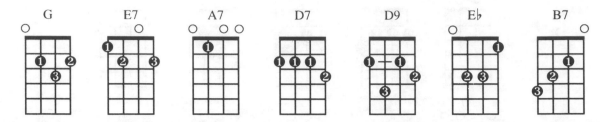

Starting pitch

I Wonder Who's Kissing Her Now

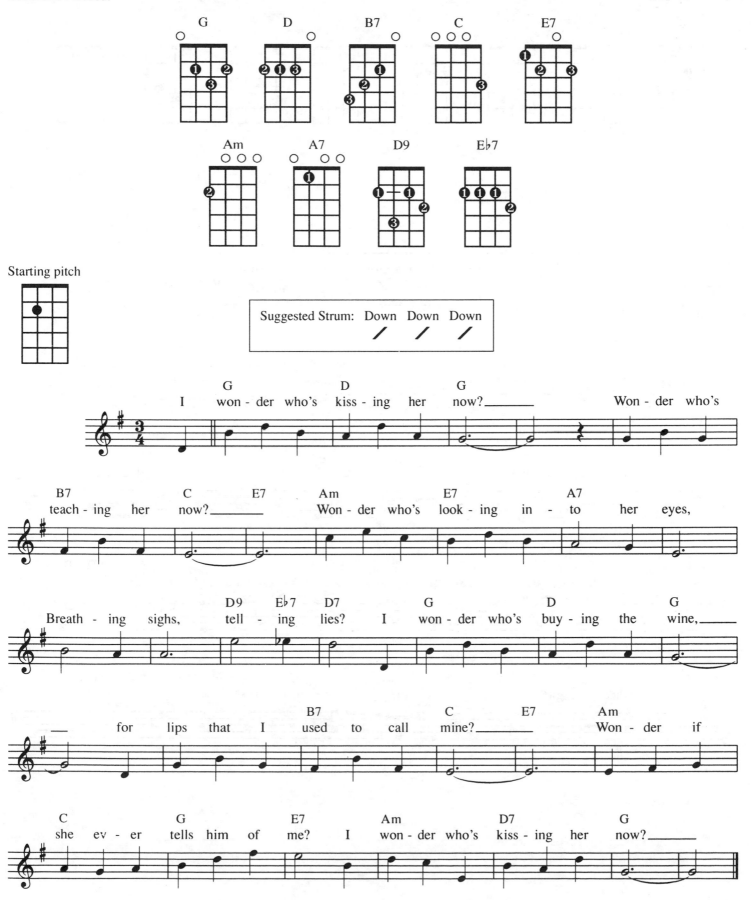

I Want A Girl

CHORDS Needed:

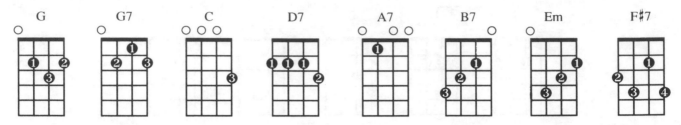

Starting pitch

Suggested Strum: Down Down up Down up Down up

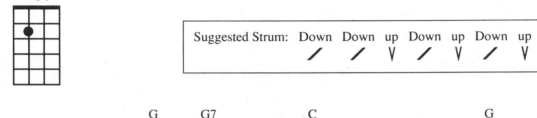

G   G7   C   G   D7   G
I   want a girl   just   like the girl that mar - ried dear old Dad.

C   G   A7   D7
She   was a girl   and   the on - ly girl that Dad - dy ev - er   had._____ A

G   B7   Em   B7   (F#7) D7
good   old   fash-ioned girl with heart so true,   one who loves no-bod-y   else but you.

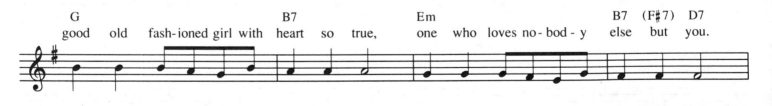

G   G7   C   G   D7   G
I   want a girl   just   like the girl that mar - ried dear old Dad.

68

Poor Butterfly

When You And I Were Young, Maggie

CHORDS Needed:

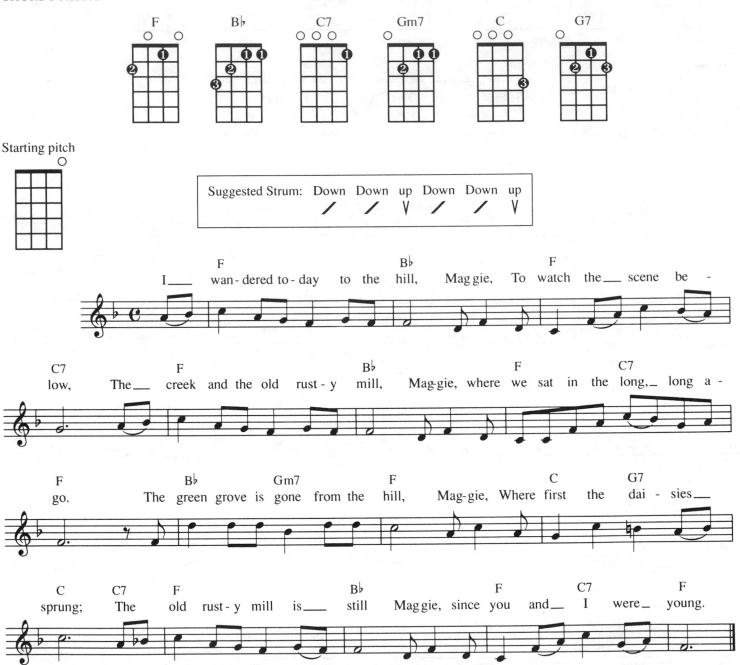

Starting pitch

Suggested Strum: Down Down up Down Down up

F
I___ wan-dered to-day to the hill, Maggie, To watch the___ scene be -

Bb
F

C7
F
low, The___ creek and the old rust-y mill, Maggie, where we sat in the long,___ long a -

Bb
F
C7

F
go. The green grove is gone from the hill, Mag-gie, Where first the dai-sies___

Bb
Gm7
F
C
G7

C
C7
F
sprung; The old rust-y mill is___ still Maggie, since you and___ I were___ young.

Bb
F
C7
F

Hello! Ma Baby

CHORDS Needed:

Starting pitch

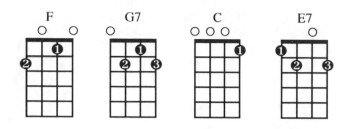

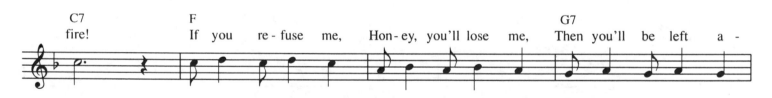

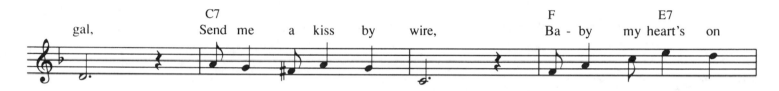

Melody of Love

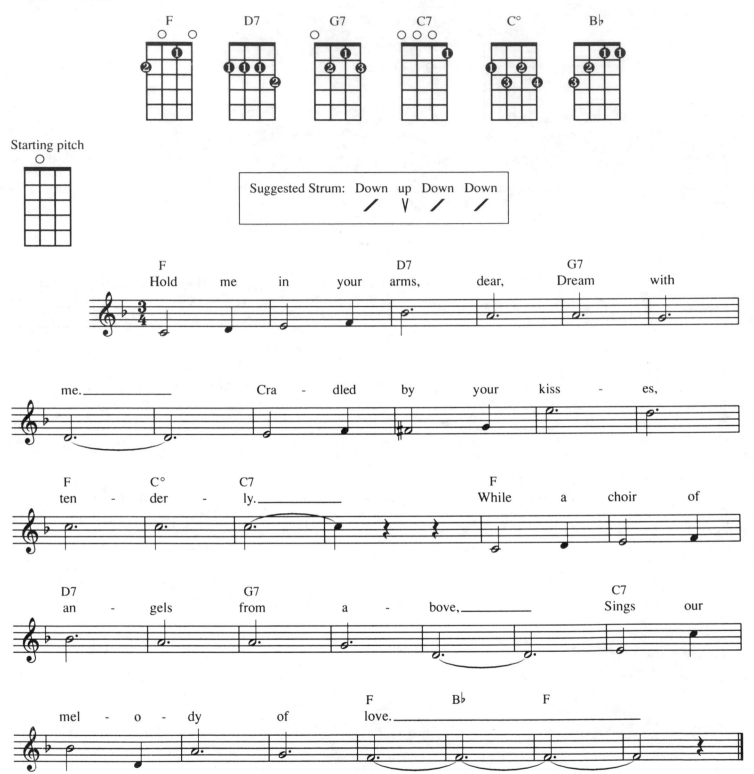

Alexander's Ragtime Band

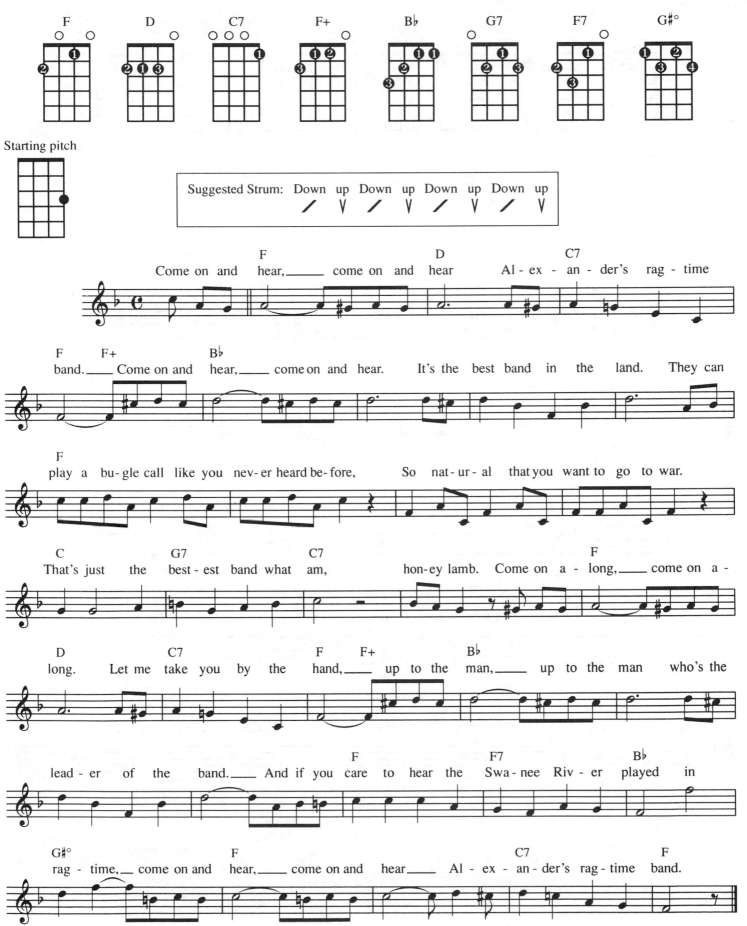

After the Ball

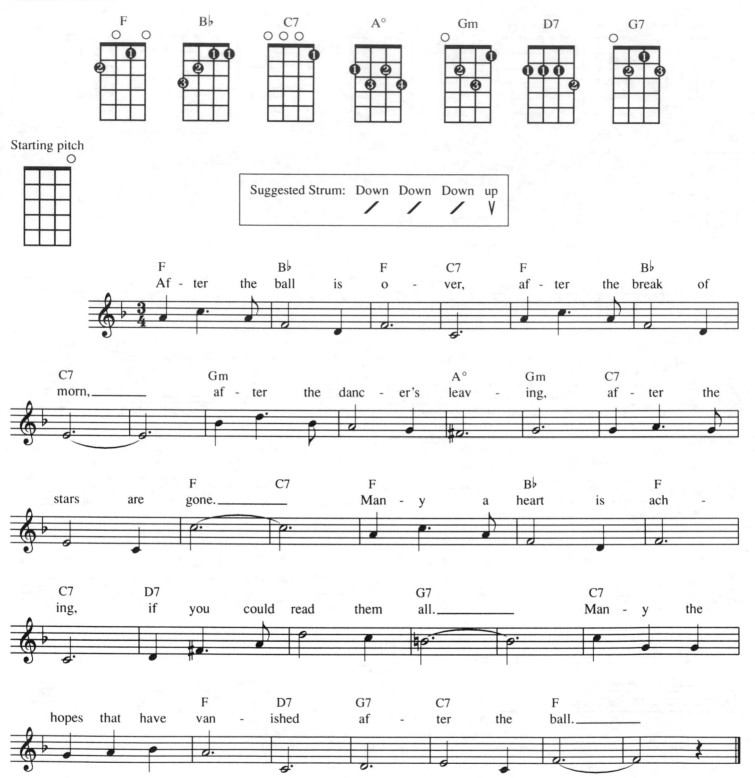

I Love You Truly

You're A Grand Old Flag

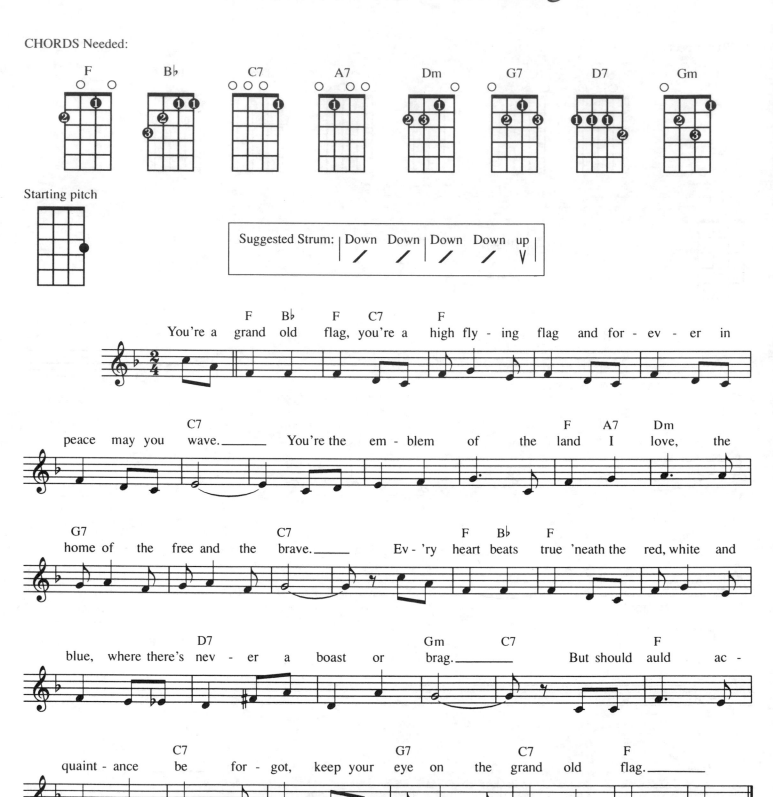

Bicycle Built For Two

CHORDS Needed:

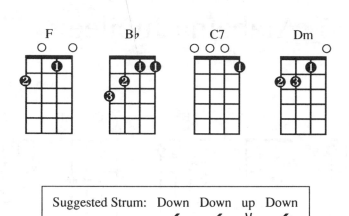

Starting pitch

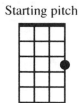

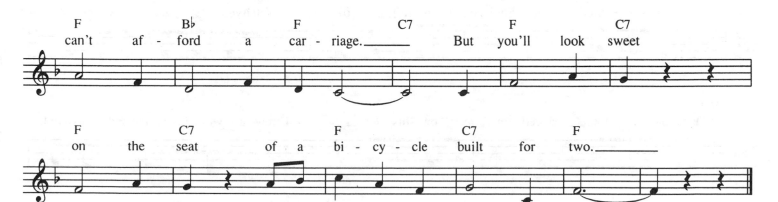

Alabama Jubilee

CHORDS Needed:

Sweet Rosie O'Grady

Peg O' My Heart

Ballin' The Jack

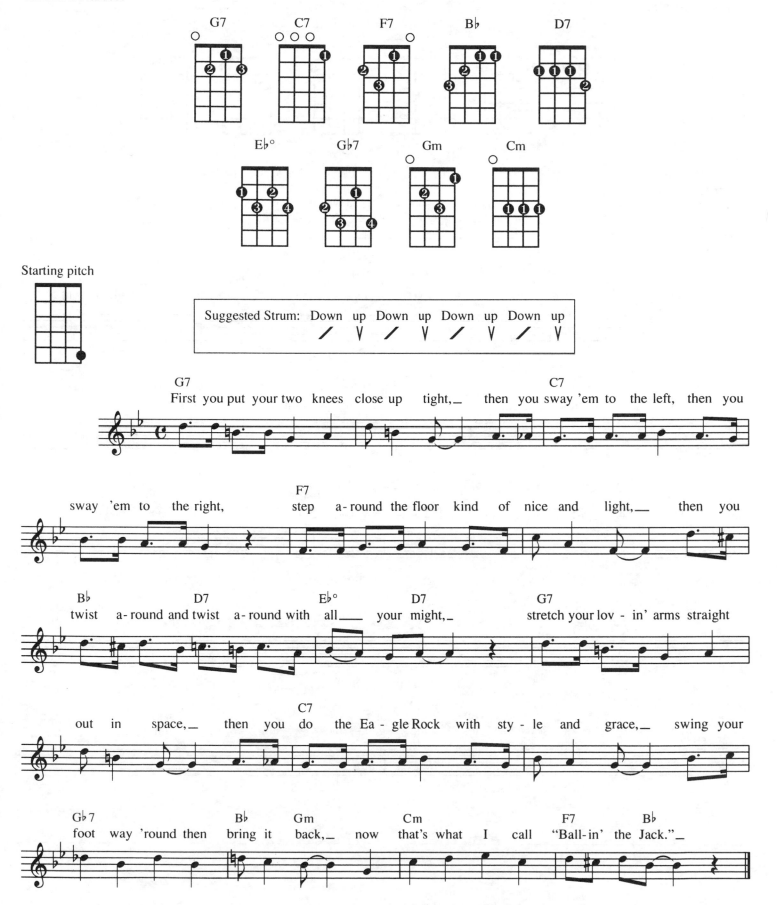

In The Good Old Summertime

CHORDS Needed:

Starting pitch

Suggested Strum: Down Down up Down

In the good old sum - mer - time, _____ in the good old

sum - mer - time _____ stroll - ing thru the sha - dy lanes,

with your ba - by mine; _____ You hold her hand and she holds

yours, and that's a ve - ry good sign _____ that she's your

toot - sey woot - sey in the good old sum - mer - time. _____

The Yankee Doodle Boy

CHORDS Needed:

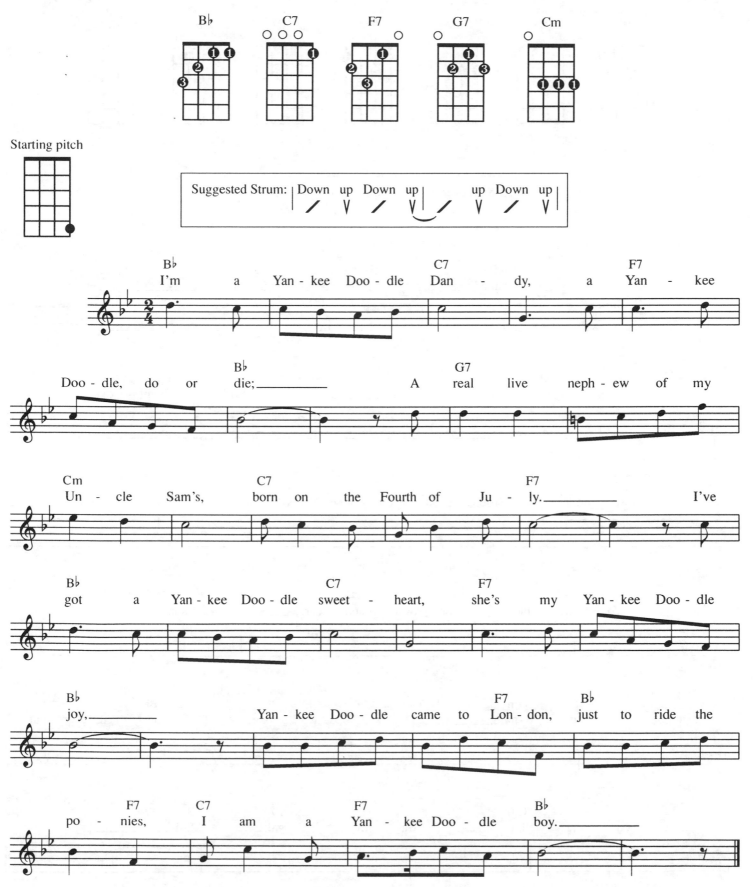

My Gal Sal

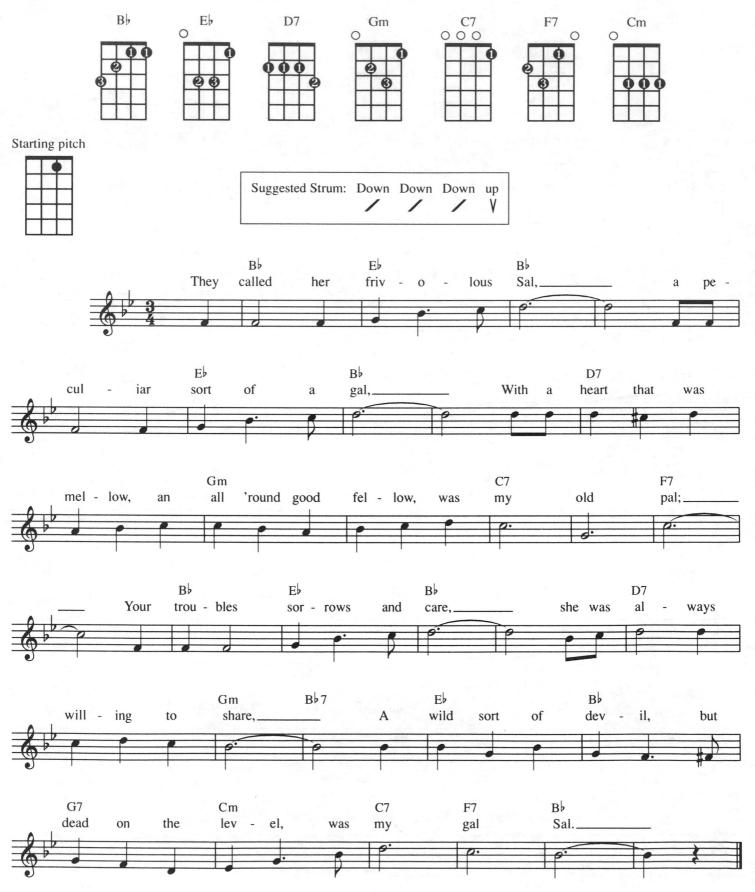

My Wild Irish Rose

Give My Regards To Broadway

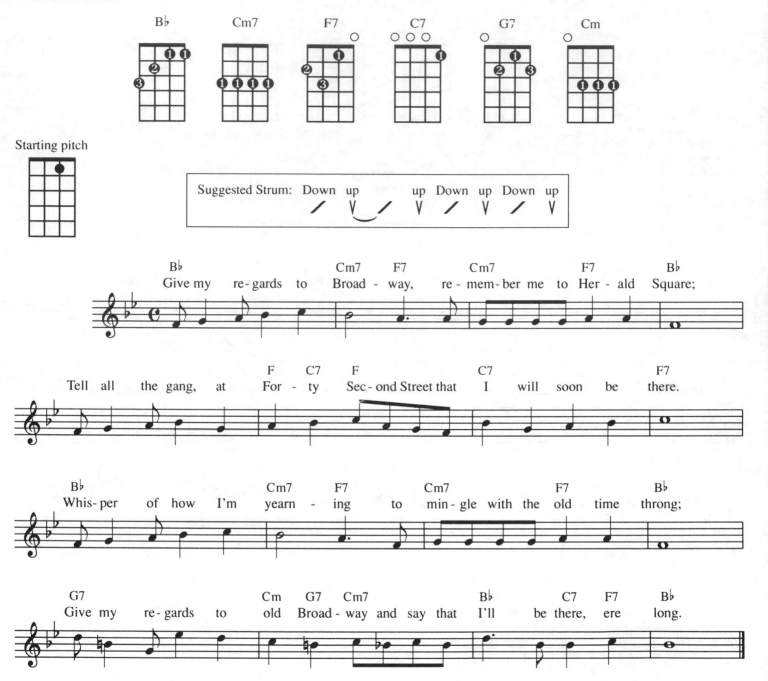

Take Me Out To The Ballgame

Let Me Call You Sweetheart

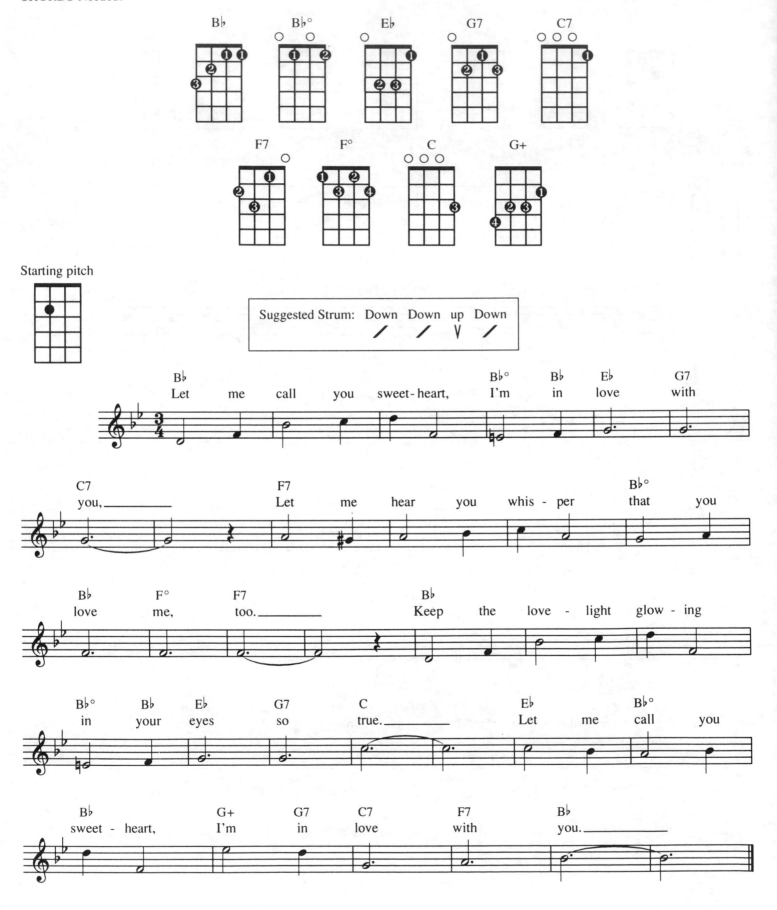

The Blue Bells of Scotland

CHORDS Needed:

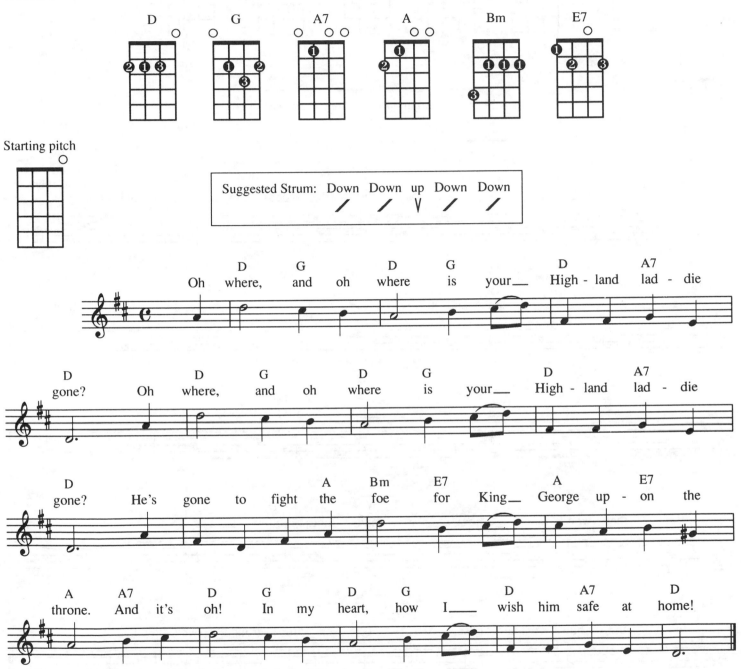

Over the River and Through the Woods

CHORDS Needed:

Beautiful Dreamer

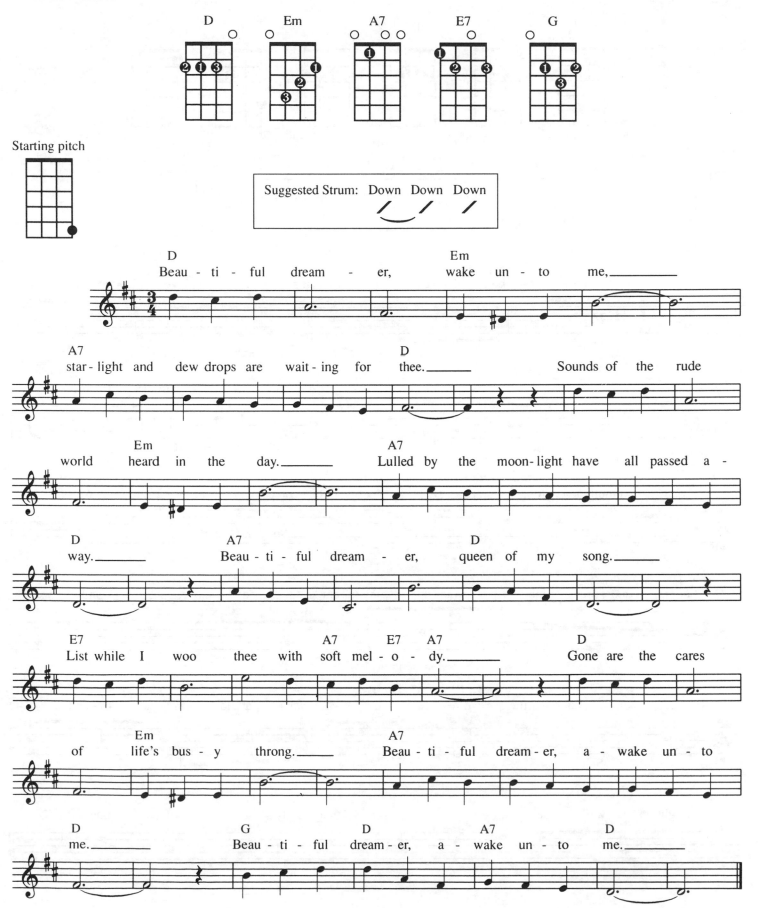

Pretty Baby

CHORDS Needed:

My Melancholy Baby

Basic Uke Chord Chart

MAJOR Chords

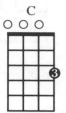 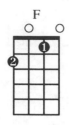 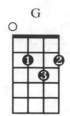  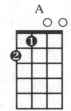 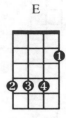

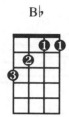 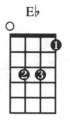 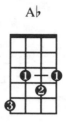 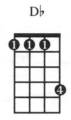 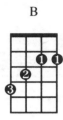

MINOR Chords

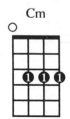 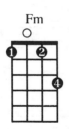 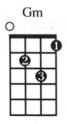 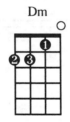 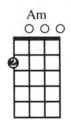 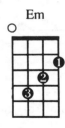

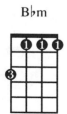 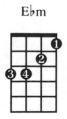 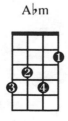 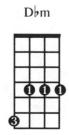 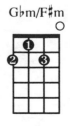 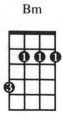

94

SEVENTH Chords

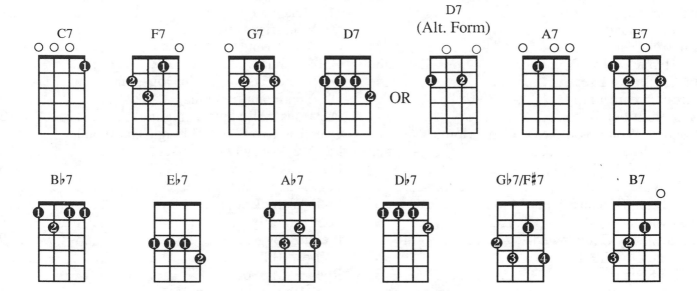

DIMINISHED Chords

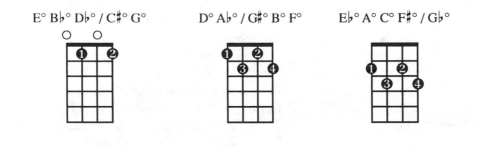

AUGMENTED Chords

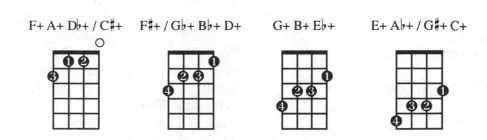

For complete Photo/Diagram Chord Listing see

Mel Bay's Ukulele Chord Book (MB 93269)

Index Of Songs

After The Ball 74
Alabama Jubilee 78
Alexander's Ragtime Band 73
All Through The Night 32
Aloha Oe 27
Away In A Manger 31
Ballin' The Jack 81
Battle Hymn Of The Republic 30
Beautiful Brown Eyes 48
Beautiful Dreamer 91
Bicycle Built For Two 77
Bill Bailey, Won't You Please Come Home? 64
Blow, Ye Winds 33
Blue Bells Of Scotland, The 89
Buffalo Gals 17
By The Light Of The Silvery Moon 53
Camptown Races 24
Chinatown, My Chinatown 50
Come And Go With Me 42
Crawdad Song 39
Darktown Strutter's Ball 54
Dear Old Girl 57
Down By The Old Mill Stream 62
Down By The Riverside 34
East Side, West Side 60
Every Time I Feel The Spirit 25
Farewell To Thee 27
Fascination 49
For Me And My Gal 65
Frankie & Johnny 42
Girl I Left Behind Me, The 40
Give My Regards To Broadway 86
Go Tell It On The Mountain 29
Goin' Down The Road Feelin' Bad 48
Gospel Train, The 35
He's Got The Whole World 18
Hello! Ma Baby 71
Hey Lolly 18
I Love You Truly 75
I Want A Girl 68
I Wonder Who's Kissing Her Now 67
Ida, Sweet As Apple Cider 51
In The Good Old Summertime 82
In My Merry Oldsmobile 58
It Ain't Gonna Rain No More! 16
Juanita 44
Let Me Call You Sweetheart 88
Li'l Liza Jane 40
Marine's Hymn, The 23
Mary Ann 47

Meet Me In St. Louis, Louis 56
Melody Of Love 72
Moonlight Bay 28
My Gal Sal 84
My Melancholy Baby 93
My Wild Irish Rose 85
Oh, My Darling Clementine 14
Oh! Susanna 41
Oh Where Has My Little Dog Gone? 16
Oh, You Beautiful Doll 66
Our Boys Will Shine Tonight 22
Over The River And Through The Woods . . . 90
Pay Me Money Down 15
Peace Like A River 32
Peg O' My Heart 80
Polly Wolly Doodle 13
Poor Butterfly 69
Pretty Baby 92
Railroad Bill 24
Rock-A-My Soul 13
Row, Row, Row Your Boat 11
Santa Lucia 20
She'll Be Coming Round The Mountain 35
She Wore A Yellow Ribbon 37
Shine On Harvest Moon 59
Sidewalks Of New York, The 60
Skip To My Lou 12
Standing In The Need Of Prayer 25
Streets Of Laredo 39
Swanee River 21
Sweet By And By 46
Sweet Rosie O'Grady 79
Swing Low, Sweet Chariot 45
Take Me Out To The Ballgame 87
That's An Irish Lullaby 55
This Little Light Of Mine 31
This Train 47
Three Blind Mice 11
Three Fishermen 15
Wabash Cannonball, The 33
Wait Till The Sun Shines, Nellie 61
When Irish Eyes Are Smiling 52
When The Saints Go Marchin' In 38
When You And I Were Young, Maggie 70
While Strolling Through The Park One Day 63
Wildwood Flower 22
Yankee Doodle Boy, The 83
Yellow Rose of Texas 21
You're A Grand Old Flag 76